BROKEN

AND

BEAUTIFUL

Visit us at deseretbook.com

ISBN 978-1-62972-798-1

Printed in China
RR Donnelley, Dongguan, China

10   9   8   7   6   5   4   3   2   1

BROKEN

AND

BEAUTIFUL

CALEE REED

DESERET
BOOK

AS A CHILD, I took many road trips with my family. I'm sure my own children would never believe that my sisters and I survived days-long journeys from California to Idaho in my parents' huge 1980s Chevrolet van without access to videos or iPads, but somehow we all managed. With four girls in my family and very few years separating us in age, we spent the hours singing "Ninety-Nine Bottles of Sprite on the Wall," making up games, and driving each other crazy.

EVERY SO OFTEN, I'd find myself looking out the window at vast stretches of undeveloped land. Deserts and mountains—miles and miles of them— ran along the sides of the freeway, lined by wire fences held together with weathered wooden posts.

If I squinted my eyes just enough and looked out at those long expanses of wire fencing, tiny, shining mirages would magically appear along the road-side, glittering brilliantly in the sun. I would often make up stories about them: they were treasure left by bandits; they were diamonds forgotten by adventurers.

AS I GOT OLDER, I realized that the treasure I imagined I had seen for all of those years was nothing but trash on the side of the freeway: broken bottles in heaps on the ground, strands of shiny plastic bags streaming in the breeze, tin cans, or broken plastic toys. Our car had passed them so quickly that I hadn't noticed the details of what was reflecting the sunlight...

. . . ONLY THAT THE LIGHT WAS
BEING REFLECTED THERE—AND
THAT IT WAS BEAUTIFUL.

FAST-FORWARD a couple of decades, to the inexpressible heaviness I felt as I finally accepted that my marriage was over. I had poured my heart and soul into salvaging it for so long that I wasn't sure who I was anymore in the wake of its ending. And I had become so BROKEN along the way.

One morning, as I drove to work as a newly single mom, something shiny on the side of the road caught my eye. I focused on it for a moment and then, realizing it was just a broken bottle, shifted my eyes back to the road. But my thoughts turned to all the "treasure" I had seen as a child, and suddenly I imagined myself reflecting light—all of my broken pieces being flooded by the light of our Savior. I thought about how BEAUTIFUL all of that brokenness could become if I invited Him more fully into my darkest spaces.

When the light shines through me
ALL THE BROKEN PIECES
REFLECT HIS LIGHT
It's a beautiful sight

All the scars and spaces
Where the battles hurt me
Let more LIGHT in
Flood me with Him

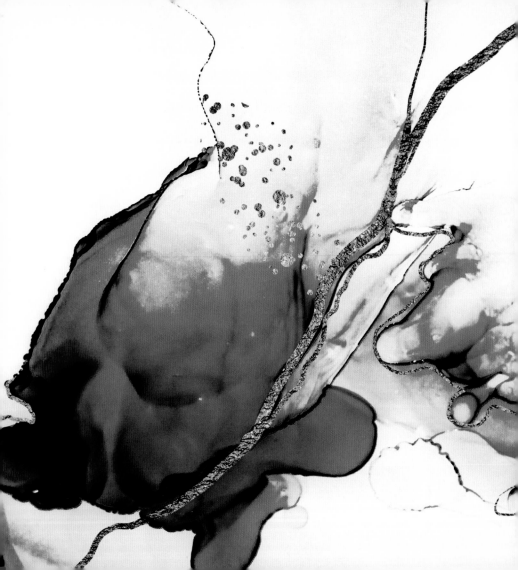

You may see
Flaws in me
I'm not perfect
But I was never meant to be

Keep your view
Of your perfect world
I was never meant to be that girl

I'm broken
BROKEN AND BEAUTIFUL

After my divorce, I spent a lot of time thinking about BELONGING. It's easy to look out across the congregation at church during a talk about the importance of eternal families, to identify how many beautiful, happy, two-parent families are sitting together on pews, and to feel like the sorely out-of-place single mom on the back row. I felt intensely aware of curious eyes, and I often felt defensive over questions or comments that I'm sure weren't meant to offend me. "Do I really belong here?" I would ask myself.

The answer has come to me in waves and is consistently reaffirmed to me when I open my heart up to hear the truth:

I BELONG TO GOD,

AND THEREFORE,

I BELONG HERE.

I OFTEN DENY MYSELF PERMISSION TO BELONG. I think we all do sometimes. We find reasons to separate ourselves because of our experiences—our trauma, our burdens, our sins. We imagine that people can't understand us because the path we've walked is different from theirs. We wait for money to be right—or clothes, or education, or marital status—before we allow ourselves to believe we belong. We wait for grief to pass. We wait for the right calling (or any calling). We wait for an apology we feel we're owed, or for someone to notice us.

THE TRUTH IS: We are known and understood perfectly by a God who knows our hearts better than we know them ourselves. He loves me (and you) not in spite of our failings, but including them. Our gifts *and* flaws are intended to help us learn and grow. He loves us. You belong *to* and *with* Him.

You don't have to *be* anything to belong (perfect, married, covered in children, physically beautiful, wealthy, educated). You belong because you are His. There is no other approval, no other acceptance, no other understanding that will ever matter in light of that truth.

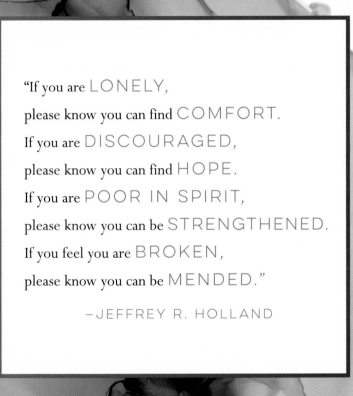

"If you are LONELY,

please know you can find COMFORT.

If you are DISCOURAGED,

please know you can find HOPE.

If you are POOR IN SPIRIT,

please know you can be STRENGTHENED.

If you feel you are BROKEN,

please know you can be MENDED."

–JEFFREY R. HOLLAND

Every shade and color
All fit together
Each break designed with me in mind

Every brilliant facet
Tells a different story
In every broken dream
His love is seen

Keep your view
Of your perfect world
I was never meant to be that girl

I'm broken
BROKEN AND BEAUTIFUL

There is a Japanese art form called KINTSUGI: "to repair with gold." It involves mending broken pottery with lacquer and gold or silver powder in the cracks. The understanding is that the piece is more beautiful for having been broken.

When I learned about *kintsugi*, the parallel of the Savior's Atonement was immediately powerful to me. His grace is the gold that runs through all of our human brokenness and makes us more beautiful and valuable *because* of that brokenness. God gave us our strengths and our weaknesses; He loves *all* of our characteristics. When we surrender all of the shattered pieces of our hearts (whether broken by circumstances outside of our control or by our own choices) to God, He can heal our hurts by pouring His love and grace into the scars of our souls. Because of His Atonement, our Savior can bind our hearts back together, making us stronger, wiser, and more whole than before.

"For a seed to achieve its
GREATEST EXPRESSION,
it must come completely undone.
Its shell cracks, its insides come out and
EVERYTHING CHANGES.
To someone who doesn't understand
GROWTH, it would look like
complete destruction."

–CYNTHIA OCCELLI

THERE HAVE BEEN TIMES in my life when I've felt myself breaking—reaching my limit and being pushed beyond what I felt I could bear.

I can't tell you how many times I've wondered if my prayers are being heard by God at all, or if they're bouncing off the vaulted doors of heaven. I've felt like I was praying to an empty universe—like I had lost my connection to the loving Heavenly Father I once knew. Those hours, months, and years have been the hardest of my life. When I've looked back, though, I've realized that maybe instead of being forsaken and forgotten, I was being pushed by God to achieve my highest expression. When I've felt like everything is falling apart all around me, those times have often led me to my most powerful moments of growth.

WHEN WE LIVE our lives centered in who we are to God (His *children*), our perspective broadens and we are able to see our challenges and struggles as opportunities to learn. We are able to see that our brokenness is part of our mortal journey and that we are not alone in our suffering. Jesus Christ "descended below all things" so He could perfectly understand and comfort us when all seems lost and broken (Doctrine and Covenants 88:6).

I AM FOREVER GRATEFUL for the Lord's infinite wisdom and grace that have carried me through my darkest moments. Even when we feel alone, my prayer is that we can remember and trust in His love.

FROM THAT
WHICH IS BROKEN,
GOD REALLY CAN
MAKE ALL THINGS
BEAUTIFUL.

I'll give Him what's left
of my shattered heart
He'll piece it together brand-new
And each empty space that
was damaged and dark
Will light up with His love and truth
Yes, that's what His healing can do

Broken
And I am beautiful
He'll use each piece
To make a MASTERPIECE
From the ashes
He's creating me

I'm broken
BROKEN AND BEAUTIFUL

"TRUST IN GOD.
HOLD ON IN HIS LOVE.
Know that one day the dawn will break
brightly and all shadows of mortality will flee.
Though we may feel we are 'like a broken
vessel,' as the Psalmist says, we must remember,
that vessel is in the hands of the divine potter.
Broken minds can be healed just the way
broken bones and broken hearts are healed."

—JEFFREY R. HOLLAND

SOURCES

"Broken and Beautiful," song lyrics by
Calee Reed and Aaron Edson. © 2018 Reed (BMI), Edson.

P. 19, "If you are lonely . . . ," Jeffrey R. Holland,
"Broken Things to Mend," *Ensign*, May 2006.

P. 24, "For a seed to achieve . . . ," Cynthia Occelli,
"How to Survive the Chaos That Precedes Transformation,"
Podcast #44, cynthiaoccelli.com/life-044-chaos-precedes-transformation/

P. 30, "Trust in God . . . ," Jeffrey R. Holland,
"Like a Broken Vessel," *Ensign*, November 2013.

IMAGE CREDITS

Background: A Aleksii/Shutterstock.com
P. 4: Plasteed/Shutterstock.com
Pp. 6–7: Ekely/E+/Getty Images
P. 9: Milaly/Shutterstock.com
P. 10: Anna_Sokol/Shutterstock.com
P. 11: Separisa/Shutterstock.com
Pp. 12–13: CARACOLLA/Shutterstock.com
Pp. 14–15: CARACOLLA/Shutterstock.com
P. 16: Anna_Sokol/Shutterstock.com

P. 19: Olha Kostiuk/Shutterstock.com
Pp. 20–21: Dinara May/Shutterstock.com
Pp. 22–23: Lia_t/Shutterstock.com
P. 24: vectortwins/Shutterstock.com
P. 25: Anna_Sokol/Shutterstock.com
Pp. 26–27: SweetRenie/Shutterstock.com
Pp. 28–29: VerisStudio/Shutterstock.com
P. 30: Plasteed/Shutterstock.com

CALEE REED ADAMS

grew up in San Diego, California, and was taught to sing by her mother at a very young age. When Calee's mother passed away in 2011 after a battle with cancer, Calee decided to write her first album, *The Waiting Place,* as a tribute to her. Since then, she has released several additional albums, including *What Heaven Feels Like, Believer,* and *Rejoice!* (a Christmas album). After experiencing the pain of a divorce and the challenges of life as a single mom, Calee married Jon Adams, a widower with four children, in 2017. She continues to write and perform inspirational music in between the joys (and chaos!) of blending a family with six adorable children.